Lesson 27

Three-letter words

1

2

3

4

5

6

7

8

9

10

11

12

13

14

15

16

17

18

19

20

⊙**Read each sentence and draw lines to the pictures.**

Three-letter words

 ① A sad cat had a bag.

 ② Can a dog fit in a van?

 ③ A fat rat and a sad cat run.

 ④ A pet met an ant in a net.

 ⑤ A red bug is wet in a cup.

 ⑥ A pink pig sat on a pin. Ouch!

 ⑦ A wet mop is on a bed.

 ⑧ I can hug the sun.

 ⑨ Bob is big, but Ken is not big.

 ⑩ Six men sit on a bus.

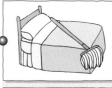

◉ 上の中で一番好きな文を1つ選んで書きましょう。

⦿Match the pictures and words. Then write the words.

1

c ➡ c + i   c + e

 都市

 サーカス

 ネコ

 ニンジン

 センチメートル

 セント

cat ➡ write

cent ➡

city ➡

carrot ➡

circus ➡

centimeter ➡

2

g ➡ g + i   g + y

 ショウガ

 ゴリラ

 巨人

 キリン

 ヤギ

 体育館

giant ➡ write

ginger ➡

giraffe ➡

goat ➡

gorilla ➡

gym ➡

3

⦿ **Complete the words and read.**

Consonant Digraphs ch sh th

1

ch

お金もちの

① ri _____

教会

② _____ ur

sh

ヒツジ

③ _____ eep

ふね

④ _____ ip

th

ありがとう

⑤ _____ ank

おとうさん

⑥ fa _____ er

2 ● Listen to the teacher and fill in the blanks.

算数

① ma _____

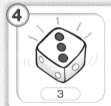
ひよこ

② _____ ick

先生

③ tea _____ er

3

④ _____ ree

さかな

⑤ fi _____

彼女は

⑥ _____ e

⑦ mu _____ room
キノコ

⑧ mo _____ er
おかあさん

Listen to the teacher and write the words.

Consonant Digraphs

 1 tree three

 2 sink think

 3 mouse mouth

 4 bus bath

 5 sip ship

 6 sea she

 7 seat sheet

 8 tip chip

 9 Terry cherry

 10 sick chick

Long Vowel Sounds　ee　ea

ee

#	日本語	問題
1	見る	s
2	会う	m　t
3	ハチ	b
4	木	tr
5	足（2本）	f　t
6	歯（2本以上）	t　th
7	ヒツジ	sh　p
8	ほお	ch　k
9	必要とする	n　d
10	保つ	k　p
11	1週間	w　k

ea

#	日本語	問題
12	海	s
13	肉	m　t
14	食べる	t
15	お茶	t
16	読む	r　d
17	葉	l　f
18	おしえる	t　ch
19	まめ	p
20	モモ	p　ch
21	話す	sp　k
22	弱い	w　k

● Complete the words and read.

Long Vowel Sounds

	雨	r ___ ___ n
①	雨	r ___ ___ n
②	しっぽ	t ___ ___ l
③	くぎ	n ___ ___ l
④	カタツムリ	sn ___ ___ l
⑤	郵便（ゆうびん）（送る）	m ___ ___ l
⑥	ぬる	p ___ ___ nt
⑦	脳（のう）	br ___ ___ n
⑧	列車（れっしゃ）	tr ___ ___ n

ie

⑨	ネクタイ（むすぶ）	t ___ ___
⑩	パイ	p ___ ___
⑪	横になる	___ ___ l
⑫	うそをつく	___ ___ l
⑬	しぬ	d ___ ___

oa

⑭	ボート	b ___ ___ t
⑮	石けん（せっ）	s ___ ___ p
⑯	コート	c ___ ___ t

● **Read each sentence and draw lines to the pictures.**

Long Vowel Sounds ee ea ai ie oa

 ① A snail and a seal lie on a beach.

 ② I see a sheep in the sea.

 ③ I can sail a big boat.

 ④ Tom can eat a big peach pie.

 ⑤ I meet a team on a train.

 ⑥ Please paint the leaf green.

 ⑦ The teacher can speak French.

 ⑧ The queen cleaned her coat.

🔲 上の中で一番好きな文を1つ選んで書きましょう。

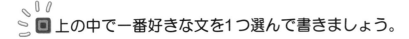

◉ **Group the words with the same sound.**

Vowel Digraph b o͡o k — z o͡o

1  room

2  見る look

3  料理する cook

4 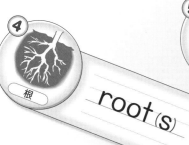 根 root(s)

5 とった took

6  すずしい cool

7  工具 tool(s)

8  ずきん hood

9 月 moon

10  足 foot

11 食べもの food

12 羊毛 wool

book

zoo

⊙ **Complete each word and copy them.**

Consonant Digraphs  ph wh ch sh th

①

oto

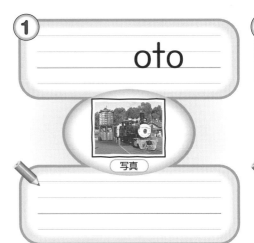

写真

②

one

でんわ

③

dol in

イルカ

④

ele ant

ゾウ

⑤

ale

クジラ

⑥

at

なに？

⑦

eat

コムギ

⑧

eelchair

くるまいす

⑨

cat

つかむ・とる

⑩

wa

洗う

⑪

ma

算数

Consonant Digraphs ck ng

● Write the sentences using the words in the pictures.

① The 🤴 sings a 🎵 .

_____

② 😊 can 👟 a ⚽ .

_____

③ The sick 🦆 is in the 🛏 .

_____

④ 😊 has a black 💍 .

_____

Silent e

1  c　n
缶

2  m　d
おこる

3  t　p
コツコツ軽く打つ

4  p　t
ペット

5  p　n
ピン

6 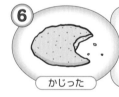 b　t
かじった

7  h　p
ぴょんぴょんとぶ

8  n　t
～ではない

9  c　t
切る

10  t　b
ふろおけ

11  c　n
つえ

12  m　d
作った

13  t　p
テープ

14  P　t
ピート（人の名前）

15  p　n
松

16  b　t
かむ・かじる

17  h　p
のぞむ

18  n　t
おんぷ

19  c　t
かわいい

20  t　b
ガラスやゴムのくだ

◉ **Write the sentences using the words in the pictures.**

Silent e

① has a cute .

② A 🦩 is in the 〜 .

③ 👧 likes to bake a 🧁 .

④ A white 🐍 ate 🍇 .

⊙ **Fill in the blanks using the words below. Then play the game.**

Silent letters  k(n) gh

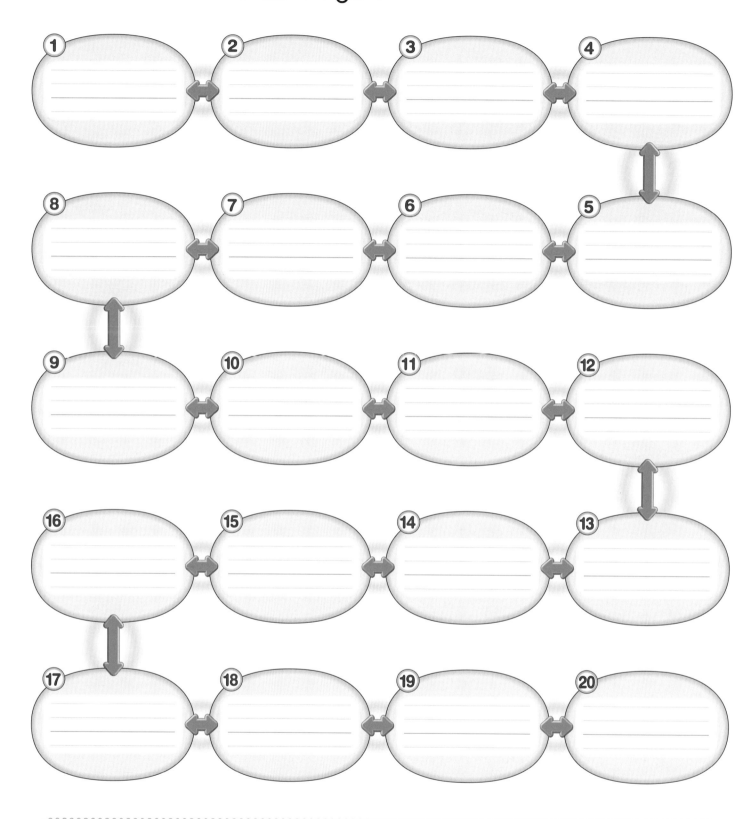

1 ~ 50 ⭐ Good.

1. ☐ bat
2. ☐ cap
3. ☐ cat
4. ☐ fan
5. ☐ hat
6. ☐ map
7. ☐ fat
8. ☐ sat
9. ☐ sad
10. ☐ dad
11. ☐ bed
12. ☐ hen
13. ☐ jet
14. ☐ net
15. ☐ pen
16. ☐ pet
17. ☐ red

18. ☐ men
19. ☐ vet
20. ☐ wet
21. ☐ fin
22. ☐ lip
23. ☐ pig
24. ☐ pin
25. ☐ six
26. ☐ chin
27. ☐ wig
28. ☐ win
29. ☐ zip
30. ☐ fit
31. ☐ box
32. ☐ dog
33. ☐ fox
34. ☐ hop

35. ☐ mop
36. ☐ top
37. ☐ pot
38. ☐ dot
39. ☐ lot
40. ☐ hot
41. ☐ bug
42. ☐ bun
43. ☐ bus
44. ☐ cup
45. ☐ gun
46. ☐ sun
47. ☐ nut
48. ☐ mud
49. ☐ run
50. ☐ mug

51 ☐ cent

52 ☐ city

53 ☐ giant

54 ☐ gym

55 ☐ sheep

56 ☐ ship

57 ☐ fish

58 ☐ mushroom

59 ☐ she

60 ☐ church

61 ☐ rich

62 ☐ chick

63 ☐ teacher

64 ☐ thank

65 ☐ mother

66 ☐ father

67 ☐ math

68 ☐ three

69 ☐ bee

70 ☐ see

71 ☐ seed

72 ☐ feet

73 ☐ teeth

74 ☐ meet

75 ☐ geese

76 ☐ sea

77 ☐ meat

78 ☐ eat

79 ☐ read

80 ☐ teach

81 ☐ peach

82 ☐ team

83 ☐ leaf

84 ☐ please

85 ☐ rain

86 ☐ tail

87 ☐ nail

88 ☐ train

89 ☐ tie

90 ☐ pie

91 ☐ lie

92 ☐ boat

93 ☐ soap

94 ☐ coat

95 ☐ book

96 ☐ took

97 ☐ look

98 ☐ good

99 ☐ hood

100 ☐ zoo

101 ☐ food

102 ☐ moon

103 ~ 150 Excellent!!

103 ☐ phone	119 ☐ hope	135 ☐ brown
104 ☐ photo	120 ☐ note	136 ☐ crab
105 ☐ elephant	121 ☐ cute	137 ☐ dress
106 ☐ what	122 ☐ tube	138 ☐ green
107 ☐ whale	123 ☐ lake	139 ☐ frog
108 ☐ wheel	124 ☐ like	140 ☐ press
109 ☐ kick	125 ☐ night	141 ☐ tree
110 ☐ sick	126 ☐ fight	142 ☐ twig
111 ☐ king	127 ☐ know	143 ☐ skip
112 ☐ song	128 ☐ knife	144 ☐ smell
113 ☐ cane	129 ☐ blue	145 ☐ snap
114 ☐ made	130 ☐ clip	146 ☐ spy
115 ☐ tape	131 ☐ flag	147 ☐ stop
116 ☐ Pete	132 ☐ glad	148 ☐ swim
117 ☐ pine	133 ☐ play	149 ☐ spring
118 ☐ bite	134 ☐ slip	150 ☐ street

1. ☐ It is a big cat.

2. ☐ Six pigs jump on the bed.

3. ☐ Wash your hands with soap.

4. ☐ I know his name.

5. ☐ Look at the big elephant in the zoo.

6. ☐ You can paint your desk green.

7. ☐ I like to fish in a lake.

8. ☐ This book is mine.

9. ☐ I am a good teacher.

10. ☐ Pete can stand on one foot.

11. ☐ A fat frog is at the top of a tree.

12. ☐ I like to read books.

13. ☐ Please stand in front of my desk.

14. ☐ I read three books at night.

15. ☐ My mother is not strict.

16. ☐ I hope to take a trip to the moon.

17. ☐ Did you see me help the old man?

18. ☐ Pete and I run to the church on Sunday.

19. ☐ I know the sick man in the bed.

20. ☐ The king and queen ate a big sandwich for lunch in the city.

★ Reading Achievement Chart ★

Completed on _____, _____ by _____.